JAPANESE DETAIL
CUISINE

Sadao Hibi

CHRONICLE BOOKS ■ SAN FRANCISCO

First published in the United States 1989 by Chronicle Books.
Copyright © 1987 by Sadao Hibi.
First published in Japan by Graphic-sha Publishing Co., Ltd.
All rights reserved. No part of this book may be reproduced in
any form without written permission from Chronicle Books.
Printed in Japan.

Library of Congress Cataloging-in-Publication Data

Hibi, Sadao, 1947–
    [Nihon no dentō iro to katachi, shoku. English]
    Japanese detail, cuisine / Sadao Hibi.
        p.   cm.
    Translation of: Nihon no dentō iro to katachi, shoku.
    ISBN 0-87701-596-1
    1. Design—Japan.   2. Tableware—
Japan.   3. Implements, utensils, etc.—Japan.   4. Color in
art.   I. Title.
NK1484.A1H5413   1989
394.1'2'0952--dc19   88-39979
                                CIP

Distributed in Canada by Raincoast Books,
112 East Third Avenue, Vancouver, B.C. V5T 1C8

Cover design by Karen Pike

10   9   8   7   6   5   4   3   2   1

Chronicle Books
275 Fifth Street
San Francisco, California 94103

CONTENTS

Nostalgia for Color and Form in Japanese Cuisine

Ayako Jindai

The monumental eighteenth-century French work, *The Physiology of Taste*, is considered by many food authorities to be the bible of the art of cuisine. Written by French philosopher and gastronomist Brillat-Savarin, it thoroughly dissects the role of dining in the pursuit of good health and happiness. The book opens with the fundamentals of preparing perfect chocolate, moves on to a discussion of the prevention and cure of obesity, and then covers practically every conceivable aspect of the culinary world.

Japanese readers may find this celebrated volume somewhat strange, however, for it overlooks what they regard as one of the most important elements of cuisine: The subject of utensils for serving food is never mentioned. The absence of such a discussion invariably surprises those who believe, as the Japanese do, that "feasting with the eyes" is a critical element in gastronomy.

The distinction between the Japanese and French attitudes on this matter put me in mind of a scene from Natsume Soseki's *Kusa Makua*. A painter in retreat from a mundane life is served breakfast at an inn and is captivated by the color of a shrimp and fern shoots arranged on a dish placed before him. He compares the composition with the relative drabness of Western cuisine, a comparison that implicitly speaks to the central role that visual sensation plays in the in the partaking of Japanese cuisine. According to Soseki, who spent some time in London as a student, presentation is of unmatched importance:

> Anything from a Japanese kitchen, be it soup, a side dish, or a plate of sashimi, is always served in an arrangement at once artistic and beautiful to behold. Just feasting your eyes on beautifully arranged food served on a dinner tray set before you, without bringing chopsticks to lips, makes for a worthwhile trip to a traditional restaurant.

But what of the opinion of Japanese gastronomists? Kitaoji Rosanjin, an authority arguably the equal of Brillat-Savarin, devoted his life to "the ways of cuisine." As a young man, Rosanjin demonstrated talents that left a profound mark in letters, seal engraving, painting, pottery, and lacquerware. Toward the end of the Taisho era, he opened the celebrated Hoshioka Tea Ceremonial Hall and established himself as a master of culinary arts, personally designing and producing all the utensils used in serving. His strong insistence was that "ordinary utensils do disservice to my food, which I prepare so carefully; it requires the proper utensils to give it life."

It is said that "if the dress is the medium for accentuating the woman, then the utensil is the means for enlivening cuisine." Equally true is that while "the choice of an unbecoming dress detracts from the beauty of a woman, the use of inappropriate utensils devalues the worth of cuisine." In this sense, Rosanjin's advocacy of specific utensils for serving could indeed be likened to the wearing of a traditional kimono by a Japanese woman.

Though not all will share Rosanjin's extreme position on this matter, many Japanese firmly believe that harmony between food and utensils is essential. Attention to the need for such balance has influenced the use of many materials, including porcelain, ceramic, lacquerware, bamboo, wood, paper, silver, bronze, and glass.

Among these materials, the most representative would no doubt be lacquerware. In many areas of the world, the very word "Japan" actually means "lacquer," and an object that is said to be "japanned" is "lacquered." Europeans effusively praised the brilliant, minutely detailed Japanese lacquerware exported to the West in the eighteenth century, and it is there that these words took on their extended meaning.

Lacquerware's place in Japan's own history goes back to the Jomon period. The Tamamushizushi shrine in Horyugi Temple is widely recognized as the oldest lacquer painting in the country, while the Shosoin repository holds a famous lacquerwork inlaid with mother-of-pearl that still radiates with the glory of the Tang dynasty.

A deep glossy brilliance shines out from layers upon layers of natural lacquer—a sheen that imparts a softness, a warmth, a sense of weightlessness. When a lacquerware bowl is filled with hot liquid, the painted surface appears almost to be breathing as the mist condenses on it.

Except for soup bowls, lacquered table utensils have all but disappeared from today's family dining tables. One is only likely to see them at special celebrations. Two examples are the luxurious *jūbako* lunch box with gold lacquerwork on a black background, and the set of saké cups and vermilion-lacquered pot brought out with the New Year cuisine. The deep sheen of these utensils seems perfectly suited to the gaiety of the occasion.

In the Shikoku farming village where I was born and raised, the custom of displaying the lacquered utensil known as the *hokai* is still practiced on auspicious occasions. The round container with three legs resembles a chest, has a capacity of about eighteen liters, and is covered in black lacquer with the owner's family crest painted on it. After the *hokai* is filled with round rice cakes, believed to bring good luck to those receiving them, its lid is secured with a red cord, and the container placed in a square box. Carrying poles are passed through the box for transporting the *hokai* to those being honored. I understand that the custom surrounding this classic chest, which was traditionally used by brides-to-be when they proceeded to the homes of their grooms, can be traced to the Heian period.

The Japanese take special note of the change of seasons, and faithfully meet each with the appropriate foods. This matching of food and season is among the most basic principles of Japanese cuisine. Seasonal utensils must be part of this match. Their selection is especially critical when ceremonial food is being served.

"Cool, refreshing food in summer; hot, invigorating food in winter": On the basis of this invariable principle, the most appropriate summer utensils are made of bamboo and glass. Mats and small baskets of woven bamboo refresh the visual sense, and convey the coolness and freshness of food prepared during the hot season. Tatsuko Hoshino's short verse immediately comes to mind: "How beautiful, summer cuisine accented with green."

By contrast, earthenware best suits winter. In the cold months, one yearns for the natural, unassuming warm color of clay. What better way to forget the bitter cold outside than to gather friends around a hearth with a large earthen pot in the center from which everyone dips out fish, meats, vegetables, and tofu while sipping saké. The unglazed pot bubbling quietly over the coals seems to draw friends together.

The painter expresses his or her vision on canvas. The Japanese chef first enlivens the flavors of nature's gifts, and then completes the artwork on the dining table in a form that is at once beautiful to behold and pleasant to partake. Just as a maestro interweaves the sounds of different instruments to form a perfect harmony, the master of the kitchen harmonizes the products of the land and sea with the utensils in which they are served.

Festival rituals and other national traditions have long been carefully recorded by the Japanese, including information on the historical presentation of cuisine. The preservation of these customs can only be viewed as a rich legacy for future generations.

Color and Form
Kenji Ekuan, GK Industrial Design Laboratory

When color is used simply as a means of drawing attention to something, the result can actually be unsightly. Indeed, both color and form today have become the facade of an unsightly environment. There is a tendency to justify this situation from a functional standpoint, but that begs a larger question; the problem of color and form—and their appropriate use—must be addressed in its own right. The shades of an environment are not merely neutral and functional; they color the very lives of the people who inhabit it.

On the surface, color seems to be easily managed, to be free for the taking. But color so casually considered becomes color for sale, and loses its deeper connection with human needs. Once, in the landscape area of Tokyo's Shibuya-ku, a bright red building appeared that surprised even those who have little appreciation of color. Rather than existing in harmony with the people who passed by, the building's color appeared to assault them. It's an experience that Shibuya-ku hasn't forgotten, and one that lends itself to a general premise: The notion that color and form can be promiscuously mixed in the interest of commercial promotion is wrongheaded.

Color, of course, can also enhance an object's form, much as people express their individuality, reveal who they are, through color preferences. In other words, color plays a critical role in telling the "stories" of both people and things. The act of abstracting color from objects is therefore a way of fully discovering the world. The wonder that Sir Isaac Newton must have experienced in the process of analyzing white light is a case in point.

Color does not only affect our response to form. Color and sound. Color and nature. Color and space. Color and time. All of these relationships can be explored, as can a more metaphysical subject—color and the human spirit.

People express feelings through language and movement, but these means are limited. Often there is no clear way to express sentiments relating to time, place, and social environment, except through a process that involves color. Color offers a vocabulary that surpasses conventional language.

In order to grasp the role of color in human spirit, the structural connection between act and spirit must be understood. Spiritual sentiment often prompts a desire for action, and for any valid act, there is a place best suited to that action—and a color best suited to the moment. A situation in which one's spirit is exalted, for example, might call for red, even blood red, while the spirit at complete rest is more comfortable with white.

What shade complements the widest variety of spiritual movements? Certainly it is the most neutral of grays. Take the shade that so preoccupied Senno-Rikyu, the seventeenth-century aesthete and master of the tea ceremony. This is not a simple gray, but rather one that is altered by changes in light and surrounding colors. Sometimes it edges toward white, sometimes red, blue, or even purple. Just as white light embraces the properties of all light, so does Rikyu's gray contain all colors.

Exaltation, rest, and change are represented respectively by red, white, and gray, the basic "common language" colors used for characterizing specific periods, regions, and cultural values in Japanese history. On a more general plane, red usually denotes human life, white is knowledge, and gray is the response to change. "Atypical" colors, evolving out of these common language colors, are employed to express the extraordinary.

The basic colors, moreover, are commonly used to represent spiritual resignation, while the atypical hues express obstinacy. The former are backdrops to the actions of the spirits; the latter may crop up in drama to convey sadness or happiness, anger or pleasure. They express spiritual conflict of some kind.

With modern technical advances, an ever greater spectrum of colors is available. While this has been called the "freeing" of color, it is at the same time the "estrangement" of color; we are losing touch with the common colors, in particular the neutral shades.

This confusion over colors parallels a period of growing confusion on the larger world stage. The employment of certain colors in the political arena, particularly, demonstrates a kind of cynicism directly related to ignorance of color's more natural role. In turn, it has widened the already considerable distance between people and their appreciation of color's power. Elsewhere on the contemporary front, the potential danger of color's cynical use in corporate identity strategies is impossible to exaggerate.

A highly developed bleaching technology is now enabling industries to deceive the population in a variety of ways. For example, consumers have been convinced that bathroom tissue must be absolutely white, regardless of its function or the elements that go into its making. As a result, things that are "truly" white suffer, the environment is imperiled by chemicals marshalled to satisfy the demand for whiteness, and the vitality of the color white itself is sapped. That is to say that the chemical processing and industrial selection of color deserves criticism not only for its detrimental health effects, but also because it reduces our ability to distinguish colors. The path of free color leads to the misunderstanding of life.

What does natural color express? What can manmade color express? What stories are told by the different skin colors of people around the world? And what, after all, does that have to do with human creativity? The part played by basic color in profoundly philosophical questions is something that must be acknowledged endlessly.

The generation of color has long been the work of labor and industry. But it is the people who use color who give it life and meaning. Thus, to reconsider the spiritual import of the color currently flooding our environment is also to reconsider the nature of the individual soul.

Since ancient times, color has been simultaneously part of the natural environment that fostered man, and part of the spiritual energy that fueled his use of tools. Neutral Rikyu gray still has the capacity to create even more colors in the future, but the pressing question is whether the human spirit will be prepared to accept them. Or are we now too accustomed to color to see its further potential?

The actual colors of walls, furniture, utensils, and even the city—as well as the spiritual color that textures our lives—must be rediscovered again and again, and attentively nourished. Human dignity is so closely related to creativity that the element of color is to be ignored at great risk. Recognizing colors—emotional red, intellectual white, vital gray, and the rich array of atypical hues—as emblems of the human spirit is a first step toward accepting color's deeper realities.

Color and Form of Cuisine Utensils

Yoshio Okuno
Chief Curator Nara Prefecture Folk Museum

When a society is on the cusp of modernization, new forms and colors begin to appear amidst the more familiar shapes and hues that have long characterized it. Most of the things that take on a specific shape are those associated with everyday life. This shape is dictated by materials. Utensils employed in cuisine, for instance, tend to be made of natural materials, such as wood, bamboo, clay, and so on. They are showcases for the art of the craftsperson.

Eighty years have passed since Keizo Shibusawa and Soetsu Yanagi made the case for identifying "beauty" in handcrafted vernacular objects. Even today, as artistry is gradually sublimated to "art," potters, painters, dyers, carpenters, and other craftspeople continue to create extraordinary articles for everyday use. These exquisite objects such as wooden cups, trays, and teacups, make use of forms and colors inherited from venerable traditions.

The power of form lies in structure, and that of color lies in its fidelity to nature. The forms employed in its traditional culinary utensils are founded on the circle, rectangle, and triangle (or parallelogram as transformaton of the triangle), while colors, which are mostly single hues, are predominantly light brown, brown, white, and black.

Contemporary culinary utensils reflect these same colors and forms, recalling the natural beauty and warmth inherent in the articles that have survived from the past. Consider the painted scrolls that were produced from the end of the Heian era up to the Muromachi era, such as "Experiences of Kasuga Gongen," "Saint Ippen," "Tengu Zoshi," and "Boki Ekotoba"; the tableware depicted in these classic works is generally circular, rectangular, or triangular, and finished in a black or brown tone, much the same as tableware produced today.

As for contemporary trends, the basic tableware shapes and colors of Japanese tradition have lost none of their appeal, right through the Meiji and Taisho periods to the present Showa era. But their fate, nonetheless, is increasingly in doubt. For regardless of tradition's persistent appeal, the material for making tableware began to change dramatically around the thirtieth year of Showa. Plastic resins have found their way into widespread use and standards have inevitably slipped. Shapes and colors that display an historical connection with the Middle Ages and earlier seem to be gradually losing their natural beauty and warmth.

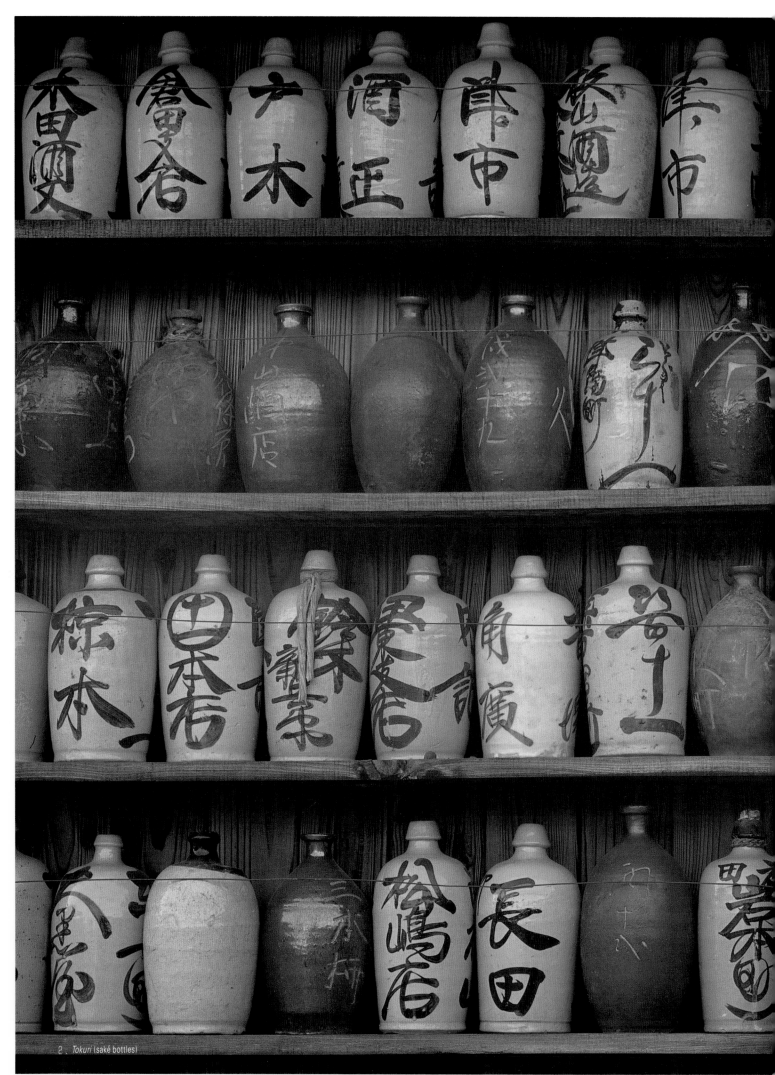

2 . *Tokuri* (saké bottles)

3 . *Chagama* (tea kettle) and *shaku* (ladle)

4 . *Komedawara* (straw rice bags)

5. *Kamado* (cooking stove)

6 _ *Tsuribe* (well and buckets)

SAKE CUPS

酒器

Saké—imbibed at boisterous parties and sipped in solitude in the still hours of the night. In the days of the *Manyōshū*, some poets were known to dispel their grief with a single swallow.

7 . Red-lacquered three-piece set of saké dishes

8 . Red-lacquered *tsunodaru* (saké keg)

9 . Lacquered saké keg

18

10. Negoro *heishi* (saké jug)

11. Negoro sake jug

12. Red-lacquered water bottle

13. Negoro *sashidaru* (saké flask)

14. Chamfered blue-underglazed saké bottle in the shape of gourd

15. White porcelain "candle" saké bottle

16. Eshino saké bottle with shallot pattern

17. Gourd used as a saké bottle

18. Large saké bottle

19. Oribe saké bottle with grass-and-flower pattern

20. Bizen saké bottle with sloped shoulder

21. Square Bizen saké bottle

22. Ash-glazed saké bottle with wide base

24. Glass saké bottle with painted figure

25. Chamfered indigo glass saké bottle

23. Bizen saké bottle in the shape of turnip

26. *Sahari chosi* (saké pitcher)

27. Iron saké pitcher with *makie* (gold-and-silver lacquerwork) on the lid

28. Wajima saké pitcher with plum-pattern *makie*

29. Saké pitcher with butterfly-pattern *makie*

31. Saké pitcher

30. Saké pitcher

32. Glass saké pitcher

33. *Kōdo water pitcher*

34. *Kōdo water pitcher*

35. Porcelain *sakazuki* (saké cup)

36. Porcelain saké cup

37. Blue-underglazed saké cup

38. Porcelain saké cup

39. Earthenware saké cup

40. Earthenware saké cup

42. Earthenware saké cup

41. Red-lacquered saké cup with gold relief

43. Glass saké cup

44. Glass saké cup with cherry pattern

45. Lapis lazuli glass saké cup

46. Glass saké cup with arabesque pattern

47. Wooden saké cup in the shape of a *masu* (measure)

48. Earthenware saké cup

49. Bizen saké cup

50. Hagi saké cup

51. Earthenware saké cup with Japanese pine pattern

52. Hagi saké cup

53. Earthenware saké cup with two distinct glaze patterns

54. Overglaze-enamel saké cup

55. Shigaraki saké cup

56. Earthenware saké cup with lily pattern

57. Indigo glass cup

58. Indigo glass goblet

59. Drinking glass with flower pattern

60. Drinking glass

61. Indigo glass goblet

62. Glass cup

63. Drinking glass with ivy pattern

64. Glass cup

65. Drinking glass with flower-and-butterfly pattern

66. Gourd-shaped indigo glass bottle

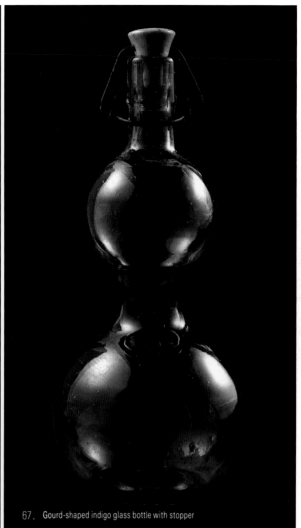

67. Gourd-shaped indigo glass bottle with stopper

68. Square indigo glass bottle

69. Glass bottle with stopper

TEA UTENSILS
茶器

The tea kettle whistles softly in the small *tatami* room. The tea utensils chosen for today have been carefully arranged. The time set aside by the host for his guests passes leisurely.

70. *Matcha* (powdered tea-ceremony tea)

71. Tea kettle of chrysanthemum type

72. Tea kettle of *shinnari* (basic form) type

73. Tea kettle of *shinnari* type

74. Tea kettle of *shinnari* type

75. Tea kettle of Mt. Fuji type

76. Tea kettle of gourd type

77. Shigaraki water jar with handle

78. Gourd-shaped water jar

79. *Hitoeguchi*-type water jar in overglaze enamel

80. Nanban water jar in the shape of *imogashira*

81. Iga water jar with side handle
83. Underglazed-blue square water jar

82. *Sendanmaki*-type-lacquered water jar
84. Water jar

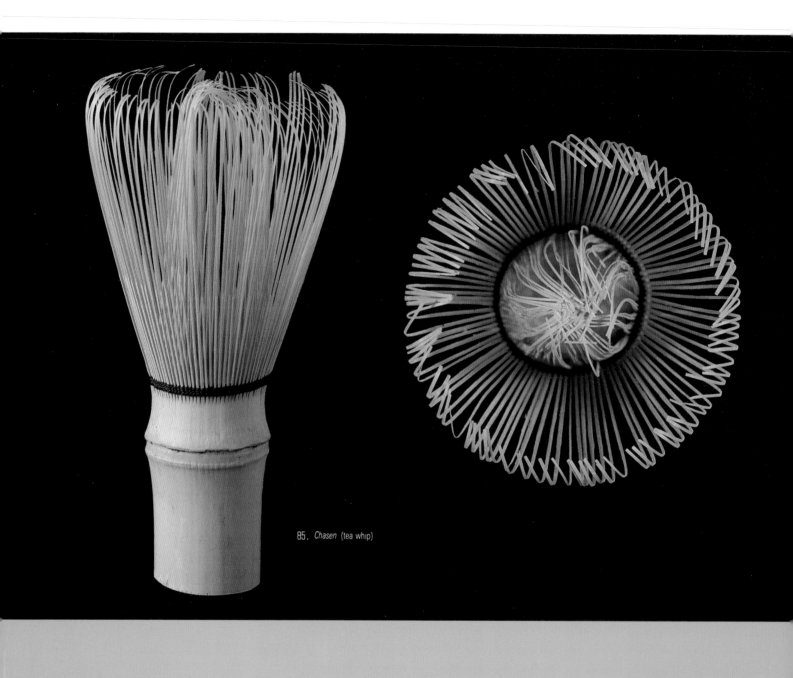

85. *Chasen* (tea whip)

86. Negoro *chashaku* (tea-powder spoon)

87. Tea-powder spoon and its case

88. Tea caddy of *natsume* (jujube-shaped) type with paulownia pattern

89. Tea caddy of *natsume* type with chrysanthemum pattern

90. Bizen *chaire* (tea container) of *imonoko* type

91. Tea container with angular shoulder, Akahada ware

92. *Shifuku* (bag for tea container)

93. Gold-and-copper tea bowl and *tenmoku* stand

94. Shigaraki tea bowl

95. *Kurooribe* (black Oribe) tea bowl

97. *Hakeme* flat tea bowl

96. *Nezumishino* (grey shino ware) tea bowl

98. *Kurooribe* tea bowl

99. *Araku* (red raku) tea bowl

100. *Tenmoku* tea bowl

101. *Kōro* (incense burner) with plum-pattern *makie*

102. Incense burner with chrysanthemum-pattern *makie*

103. Incense burner with bellflower-pattern *makie* of *akoda* type

104. Incense burner with pine-pattern *makie* and groove around the center

105. Incense burner with autumn grass pattern in *makie* and groove around the center

106. Gold-and-copper incense burner with handle

107. Incense burner of hand-molded pottery

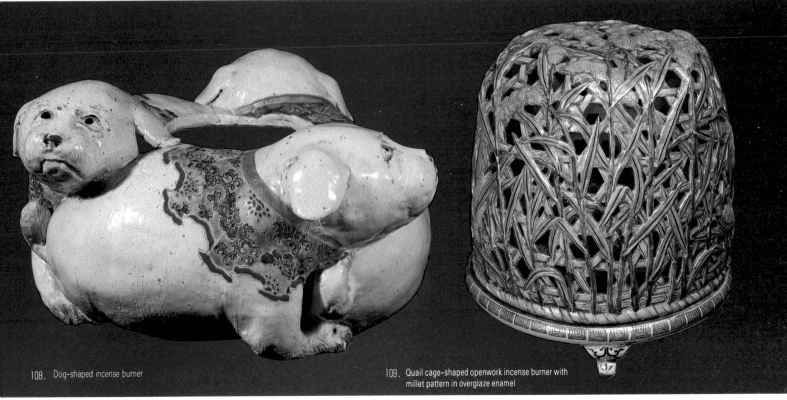

108. Dog-shaped incense burner

109. Quail cage–shaped openwork incense burner with
millet pattern in overglaze enamel

45

110. Bird-shaped *kōgō* (incense holder)

111. Duck-shaped incense holder in overglaze enamel

112. Lacquered incense holder of *Ichimonji* type

113. *Koma* incense holder

114. *Zonsei* lacquered incense holder with picture of grasshopper in relief

LACQUER AND PORCELAIN BOWLS

椀・碗

White rice served steaming in a porcelain bowl and *misoshiru* (soybean paste soup) in a lacquer bowl are the two things without which a Japanese meal simply would not be complete.

115. Lacquered bowl with crane and *ichimatsu* pattern

47

116. Blue-underglazed rice bowl with "octopus" arabesques

117. Rice bowl with animal pattern in overglaze enamel

118. Blue-underglazed rice bowl with pine pattern

119. Blue-underglazed rice bowl with dragon pattern

120. Rice bowl with camellia pattern in overglaze enamel

121. Blue-underglazed rice bowl with pine pattern

122. Rice bowl with wheat-straw pattern

51

123. Lacquered bowl with lily pattern in *makie*

124. Red-lacquered bowl

125. Hidehira lacquered bowl

126. Lacquered bowl with golden vertical stripes pattern

53

127. Negoro lacquered bowl

128. Wajima lacquered *haisen* (bowl containing water for washing saké cups)

129. Negoro lacquered rice bowl

131. Red-lacquered stacked three-bowl set (upper)

130. Red-lacquered stacked four-bowl set

132. Red-lacquered stacked three-bowl set (middle)

133. Red-lacquered stacked three-bowl set (base)

134. *Hidehira* lacquered bowl

135. Lacquered bowl of cylindrical type

136. Lacquered bowl with grass-and-flower pattern

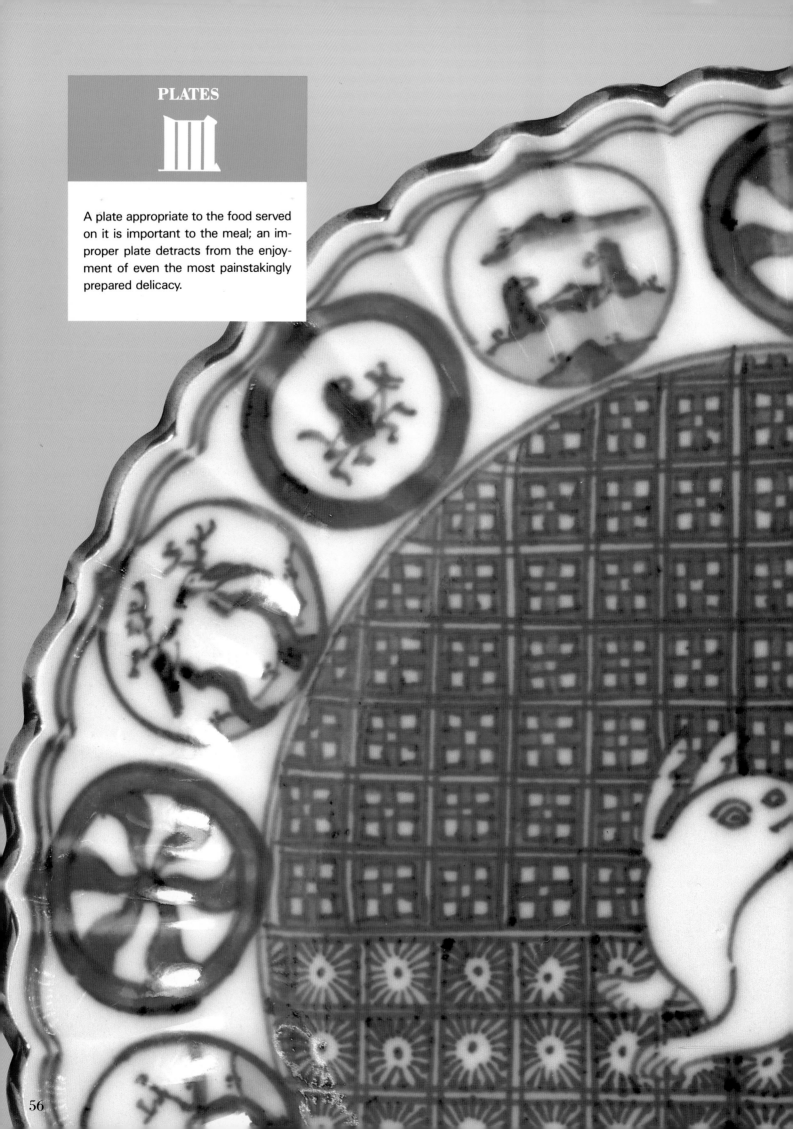

PLATES

A plate appropriate to the food served on it is important to the meal; an improper plate detracts from the enjoyment of even the most painstakingly prepared delicacy.

137. Blue-underglazed flower-shaped plate with rabbit pattern

138. Lacquered plate with Edo-period scene

139. *Umanomezara* ("horse's eye" plate) with drawing of rabbit

140. Kutani plate with flower-and-bird pattern

141. Painted plate with a rose

142. Blue-underglazed plate with landscape pattern and rust-glazed edge

143. Blue-underglazed flower-shaped plate
with pine-bamboo-plum pattern

144. Blue-underglazed flower-shaped plate
with "octopus" arabesques

145. *Dōban sometsuke* (blue-underglazed in copper plate process) with
drawing of chrysanthemums and phoenix

146. Flower-shaped plate with pine-bamboo-plum pattern in overglaze enamel

147. Blue-underglazed (copper plate process) plate with drawing of Aizuwakamatsu Castle

148. Square plate with lilies in overglaze enamel

149. Blue-underglazed rectangular plate with picture of waves and rabbits

150. Plate with pine-bamboo-plum pattern and phoenix in overglaze enamel

151. Blue-underglazed rectangular plate with "octopus" arabesques

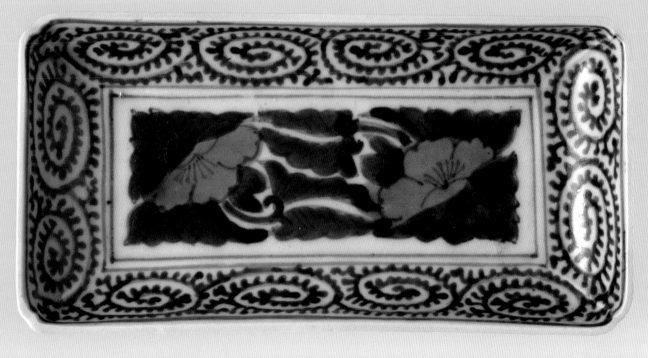

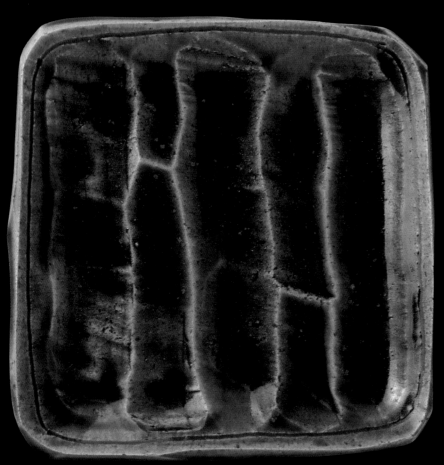

152. Ridged green-glazed square plate

153. Square Oribe plate

MAMEZARA

豆皿

The *mamezara*—a miniature dish for when you want just one more thing, for seasonings, for side dishes. The *mamezara's* size allows it to make its way around the table with ease.

154. Green-glazed plate in the shape of a carp

155. Blue-underglazed plate in the shape of an urn

156. Green-glazed plate in the shape of a chrysanthemum

157. Blue-underglazed plate with drawing of a shrimp

159. Blue-underglazed plate in the shape of Mt. Fuji

158. Blue-underglazed (copper plate process) plate in the shape of a flag

160. Thin plate in the shape of a fan

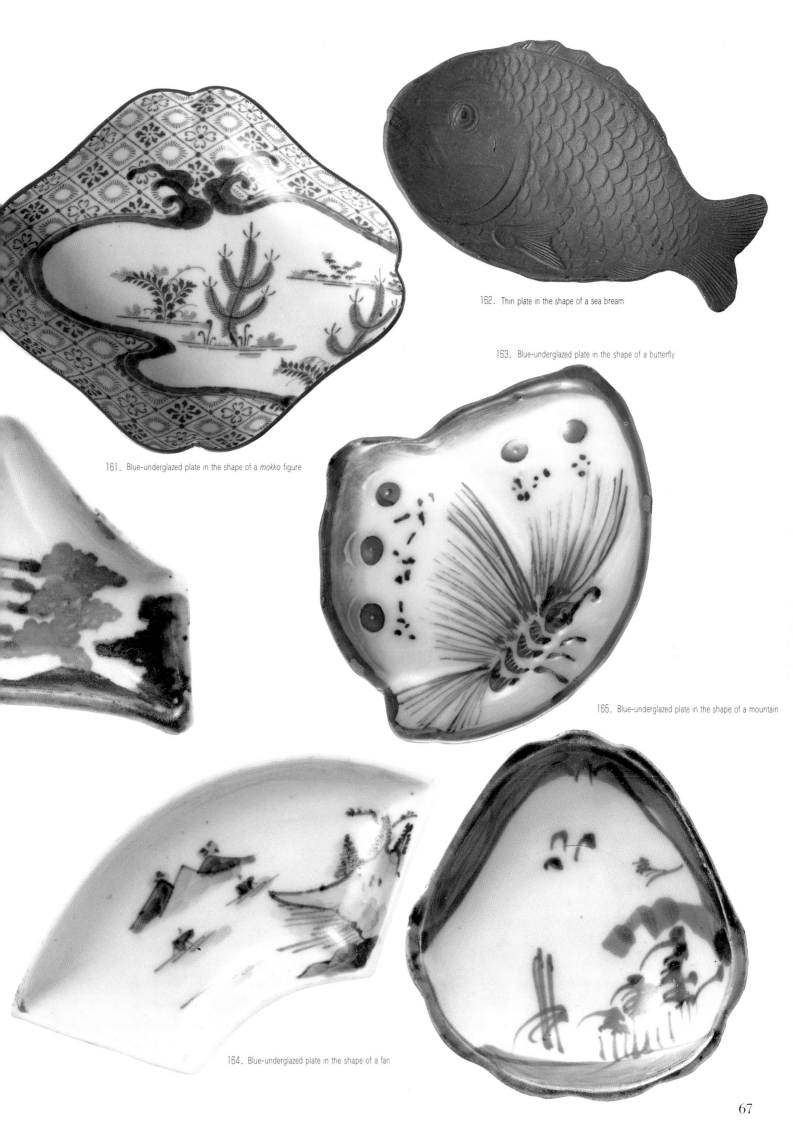

162. Thin plate in the shape of a sea bream

163. Blue-underglazed plate in the shape of a butterfly

161. Blue-underglazed plate in the shape of a *mokko* figure

165. Blue-underglazed plate in the shape of a mountain

164. Blue-underglazed plate in the shape of a fan

166. Blue-underglazed flower-shaped
plate with maple pattern

167. Blue-underglazed flower-shaped *mamezara*
(small plate) with grasses pattern

168. Blue-underglazed plate with a pattern of autumn grasses

169. Blue-underglazed rectangular small plate with a picture of Miho-no-matsubara

170. Blue-underglazed small plate with a picture of a morning glory

TSUBO AND JARS

壺・甕

The other world, or at least the pleasure of forgetting this one, is ''the heaven inside a *tsubo*,'' so the saying goes. Such a place may well be found inside a large, bottomless, enchanting Iga or Shigaraki *tsubo*.

171 Shigaraki *uzukumaru* (squat) *tsubo* (pot, urn)

172. Shigaraki large *tsubo*

173. Shigaraki *uzukumaru tsubo*

174. Tokoname large *tsubo*

175. Large ash-glazed *kame* (pot)

176. Red-clay Tanba pot

177. Large Tanba pot with running black glaze

178. Painted chamfered *tsubo* with a lid

179. Lapis lazuli–glazed *tsubo* with a lid

180. Small pot with a lid

181. Small pot with a lid

BOWLS

鉢

Bowls come in all sizes and shapes and are used for numerous purposes— from the begging bowl of a mendicant priest to dishes for sweets. These small bowls, colorful and elaborately designed, are a very important part of Japanese cuisine.

182. *Kashi-ki* (sweets bowl) with a pattern of crests in *makie*

183. Nezumishino *mukozuke* (small dish for certain foods in a formal Japanese meal)

184. Bowl with "three-fruits" pattern in overglaze enamel

185. Bizen *dora-bachi* (gong-shaped bowl)

186. *Kashi-bachi* (sweets bowl) in the *shippo-tsunagi* (overlapping ovals) pattern

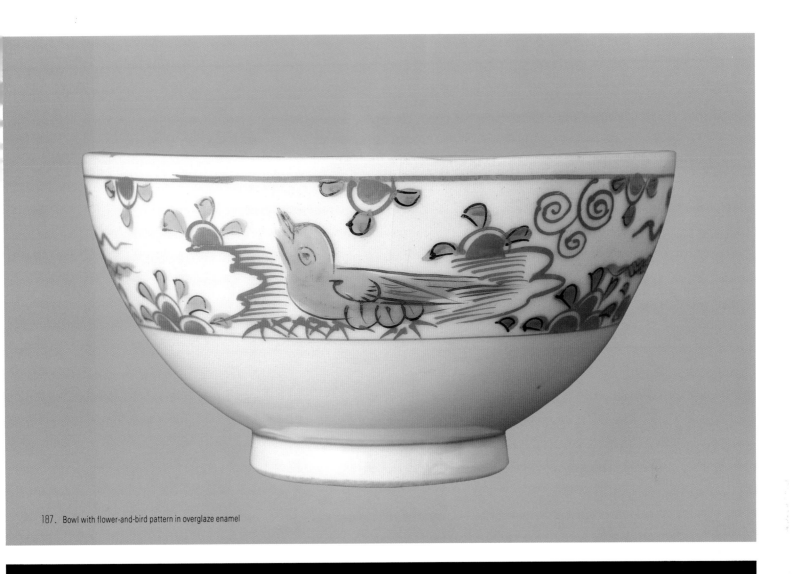

187. Bowl with flower-and-bird pattern in overglaze enamel

188. Oribe *mukozuke* with feet

189. Bowl with flower-and-bird pattern in overglaze enamel

190. Bowl with lid in overglaze enamel

191. Yellow glass bowl

192. Glass bowl with a lid

193. Blue-underglazed small, square bowl with heron pattern

194. *Mukozuke* of *tsutsu* (tall, cylindrical) type

195. Spice dish

196. Shigaraki *mukozuke* in the shape of split-prickly-ash-pod

197. Blue-underglazed bowl with waves-and-plovers pattern

198. Bowl with handle

199. Negoro bowl with "wrapped" edge

200. Negoro *takatsuki* (food stand)

201. Negoro *takasara* (raised tray)

202. Negoro food stand

203. Negoro raised tray

204. Negoro food stand

TEACUPS AND TEAPOTS

湯呑

"Tea is served!" The family members take a moment off from their work and gather together. Tea fresh from the pot and teacups uplifted—a satisfying and relaxing time.

205. *Kyusu* (teapot), Onda ware

206. *Kodo* teapot

207. *Kodo* teapot

208. Teapot with flower pattern in overglazed enamels

209. Bizen teapot

210. Blue-underglazed teapot

211. Onda teapot

212. Akazu clay teapot with chrysanthemum pattern

213. Shigaraki *yunomi* (teacup)

214. Teacup with grass-and-flower pattern in blue underglaze

215. Blue-underglazed teacup with landscape pattern

216. Celadon porcelain teacup

217. Teacup with lily pattern

218. Blue-underglazed teacup with splashed pattern

219. Blue-underglazed teacups

220. Blue-underglazed teacup

221. Shino teacup with water-plantain pattern

222. Blue-underglazed teacup with *seigaiha* (overlapping waves) and *ichimatsu* (checked) patterns

223. Shino teacup with wheat-straw pattern

224. Celadon porcelain cylindrical teacup

225. Spatula-carved cylindrical teacup

226. Cylindrical teacup with flying cranes painted in gold

227. *Chataku* (teacup saucers)

SERVING AND DINNER TRAYS
盆・膳

A typical Japanese banquet scene would be dinner trays neatly lined up in a *tatami* room. Vermilion, black, gold-and-silver-raised. A well-to-do host might serve a meal on several kinds of vividly lacquered trays.

228. *Oshiki* (square tray with edges) and lacquered bowl

229. *Zen* (dinner tray) with legs

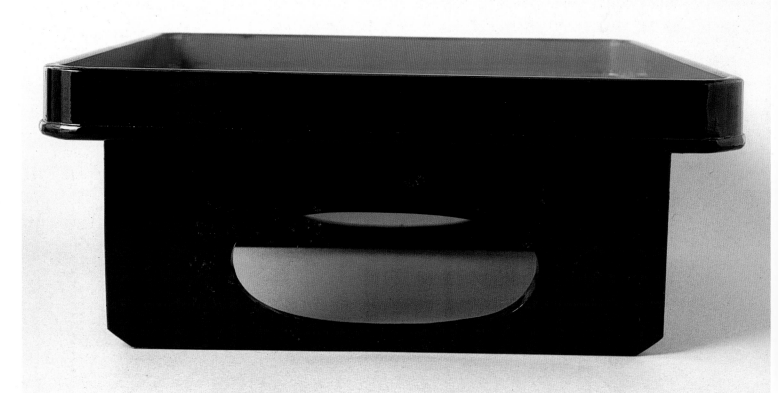

230. Dinner tray

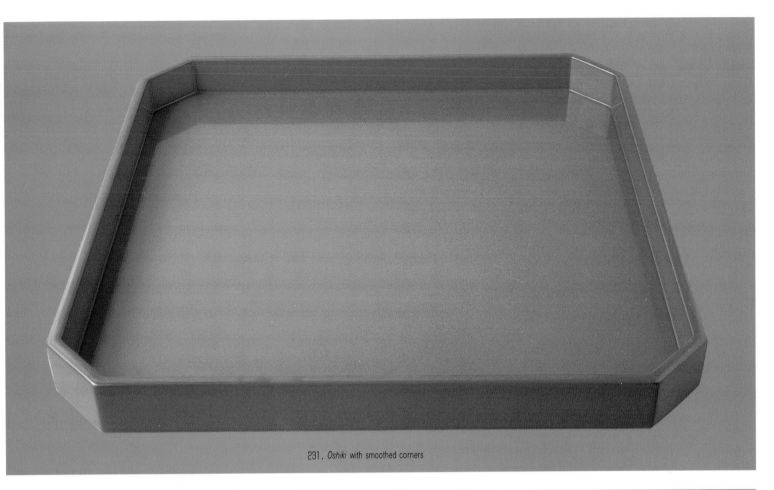

231. *Oshiki* with smoothed corners

232. *Oshiki* with smoothed corners

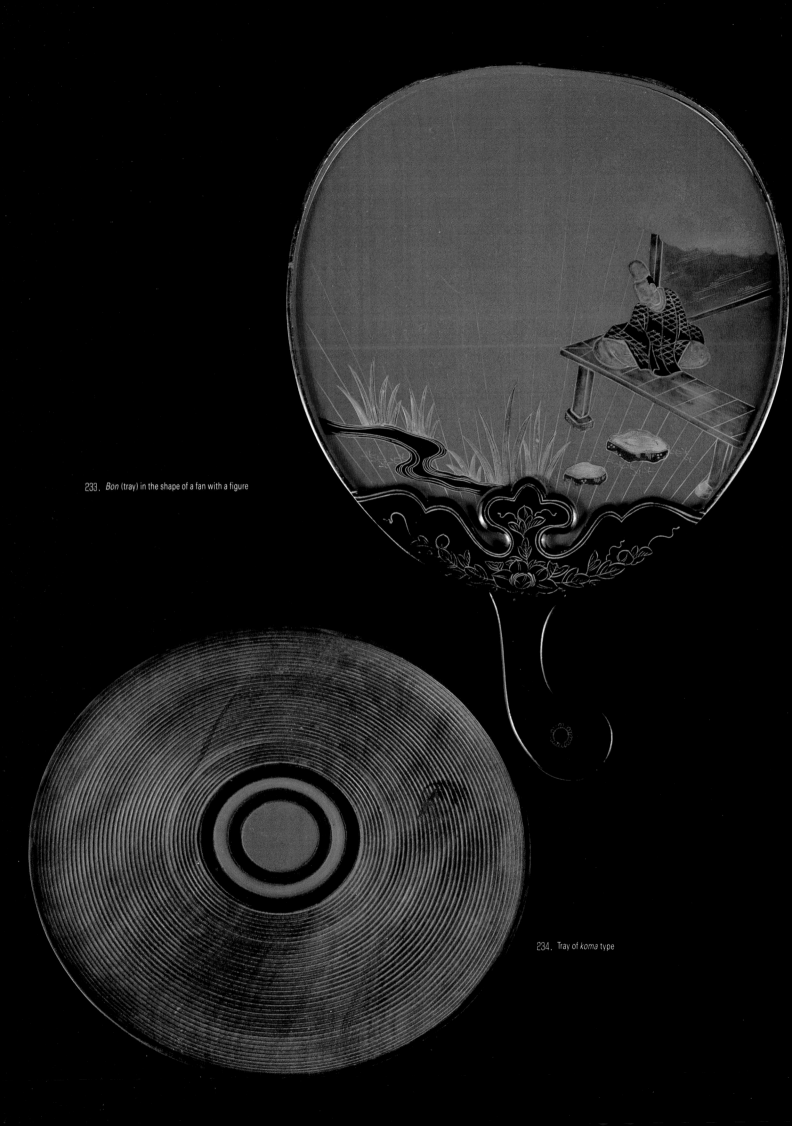

233. *Bon* (tray) in the shape of a fan with a figure

234. Tray of *koma* type

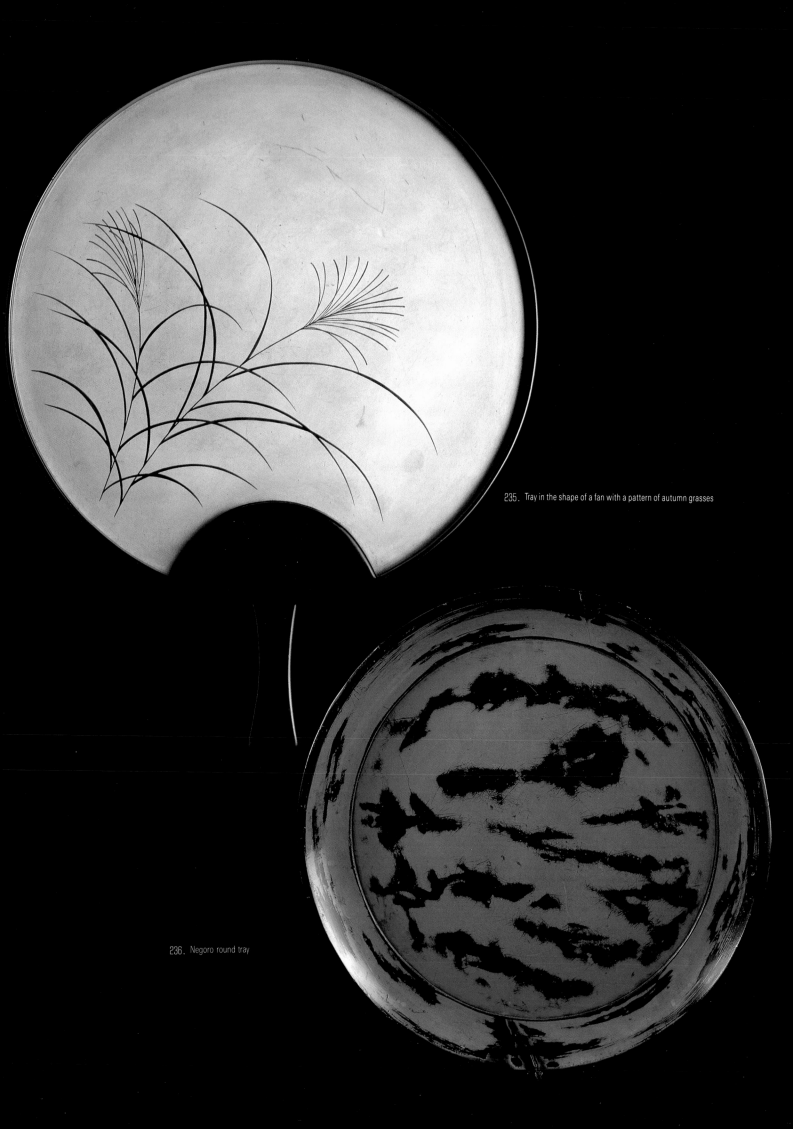

235. Tray in the shape of a fan with a pattern of autumn grasses

236. Negoro round tray

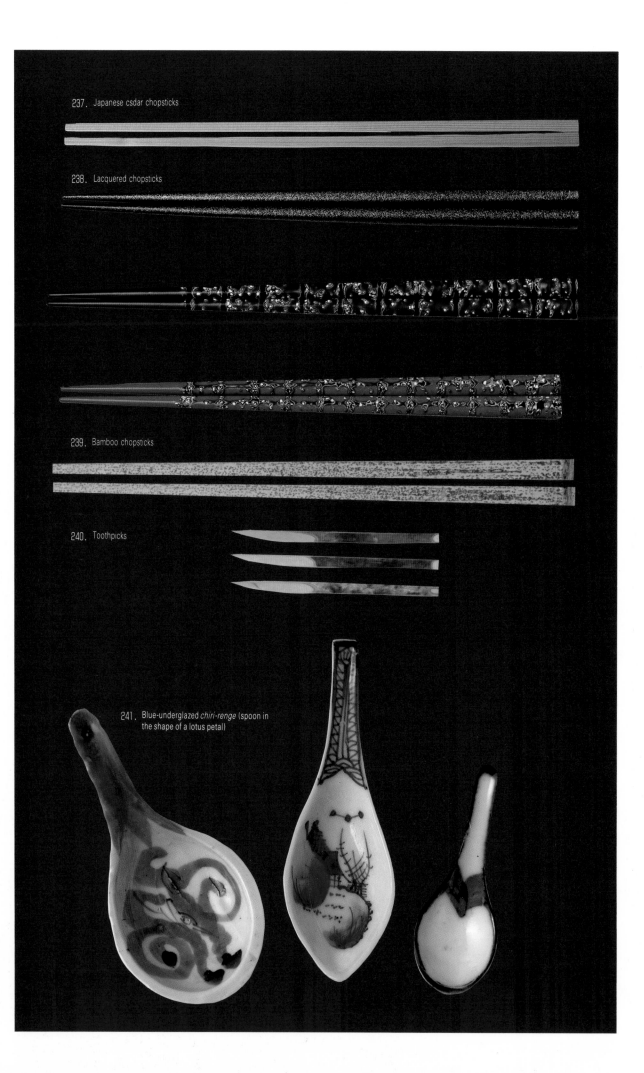

237. Japanese csdar chopsticks

238. Lacquered chopsticks

239. Bamboo chopsticks

240. Toothpicks

241. Blue-underglazed *chiri-renge* (spoon in the shape of a lotus petal)

JŪBAKO

重箱

A *jūbako* is a tiered set of boxes used to serve special foods on festive occasions: *osechi* cuisine at the New Year, meals for cherry blossom viewing, red and white rice cakes for celebration.

242. Round *jūbako* (nest of boxes) in *makie*

243. Red-lacquered lunch boxes

244. Lunch boxes with clematis pattern in *makie*

245. *Jūbako* with grass-and-flower pattern in *makie*

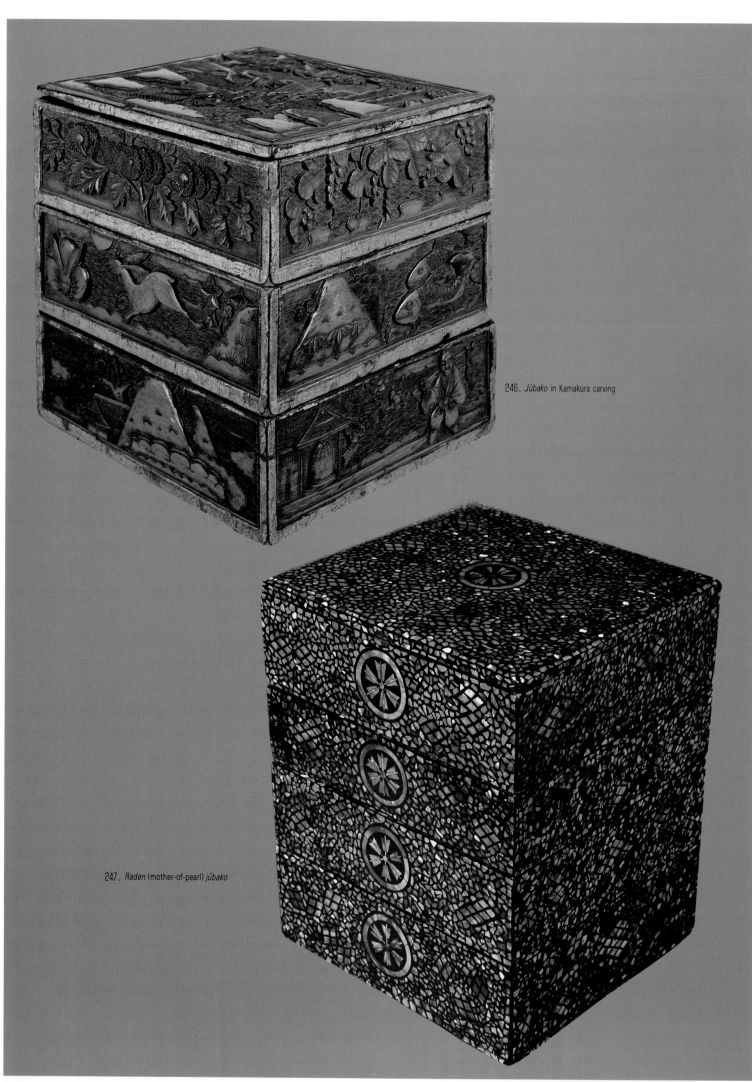

246. *Jūbako* in Kamakura carving

247. *Raden* (mother-of-pearl) *jūbako*

248. Egg-shaped *jūbako* with chrysanthemum pattern in *makie*

249. *Jūbako* with figures of shells in *makie*

250. Round *jūbako* with grass-and-flower pattern in *makie*

251. Round *jūbako* in *makie*

252. *Shunkei*-lacquered *jūbako*

LIPPED BOWLS

片口

No one pays attention to the act of pouring because it is repeated so many times each day. These handy lipped bowls used for pouring are simple, yet they possess a certain beauty in their simplicity.

253. Negoro *katakuchi* (bowl with a spout)

254. Red-lacquered *yutō* (pitcher for after-meal hot tea)

255. Soup pitcher with autumn grasses pattern in *makie*

256. *Yutō* with sea pattern in *makie*

257. Negoro *hanzo* (water pitcher with handle)

258. Red-lacquered *katakuchi*

259. Lacquered *katakuchi*

109

260. Earthenware *katakuchi*

261. Earthenware *yuzamashi* (vessel for cooling hot water)

262. Clay teapot

264. Blue-underglazed *soba-choko* with checked pattern

263. Blue-underglazed *soba-choko* (cup containing the soup for *soba*, or buckwheat noodles) with oval pattern

266. Blue-underglazed *soba-choko* with dragonfly pattern

265. Blue-underglazed *soba-choko* with bamboo pattern

267. Black-lacquered tub with legs

268. Negoro tub with legs

269. Hexagonal Negoro tub with legs

270. Negoro tub for prepared dishes

271. Wooden bucket

COOKING UTENSILS

料理道具

If the table is the stage on which a meal is performed, then the kitchen is the dressing room. Here is where the various utensils do their work—cutting, simmering, boiling.

272. Cooking stove and rice kettle

273. Rice-kettle and steaming basket

274. Iron pot

275. Rice kettle

117

276. Bamboo *tsugura* (basket for keeping a rice tub warm)

277. Straw *tsugura*

278. Red-lacquered rice tub

279. Lacquered rice tub

280. Rice tub

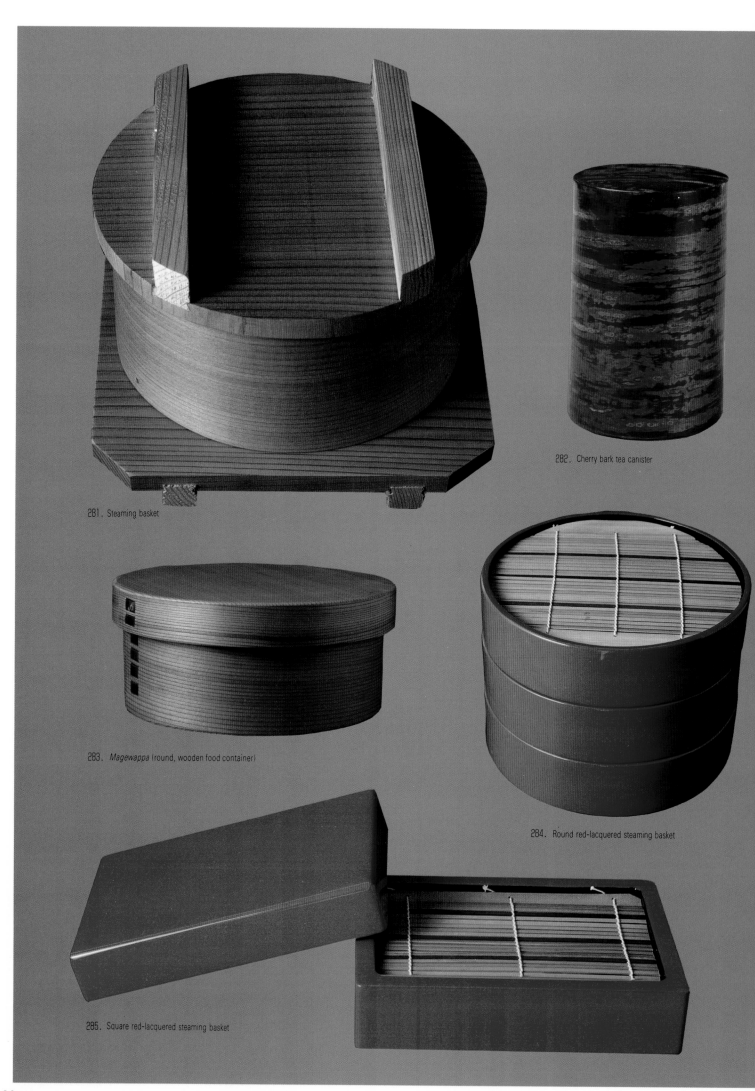

281. Steaming basket

282. Cherry bark tea canister

283. *Magewappa* (round, wooden food container)

284. Round red-lacquered steaming basket

285. Square red-lacquered steaming basket

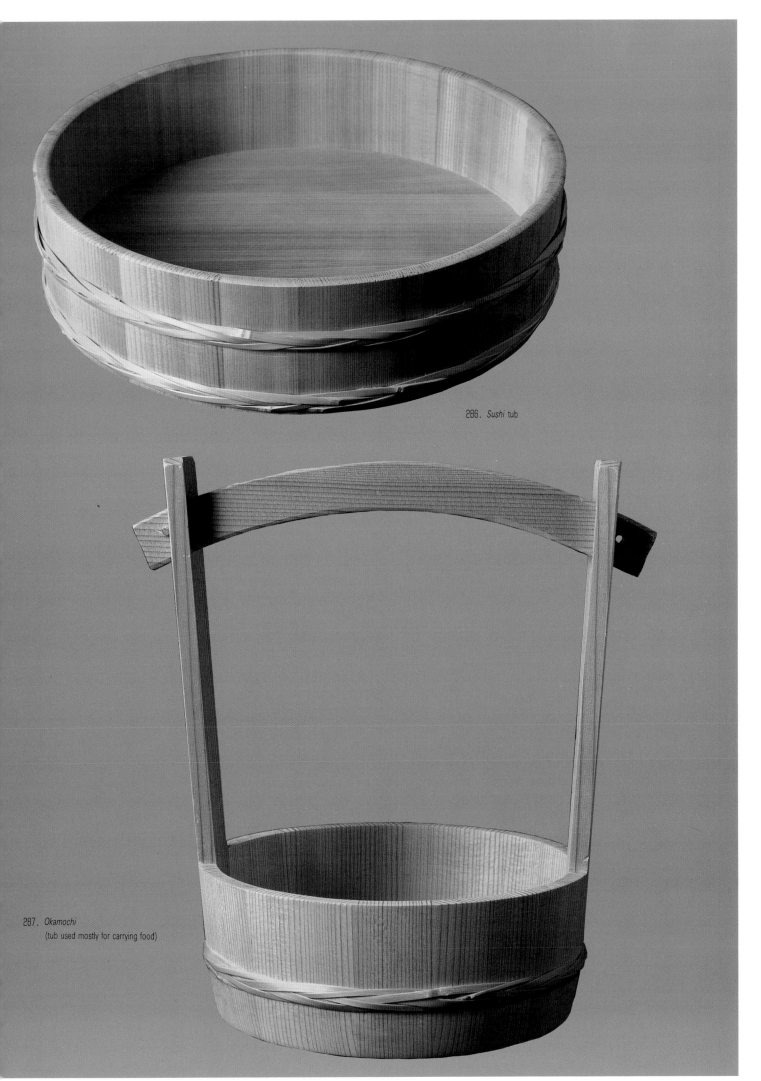

286. *Sushi* tub

287. *Okamochi*
(tub used mostly for carrying food)

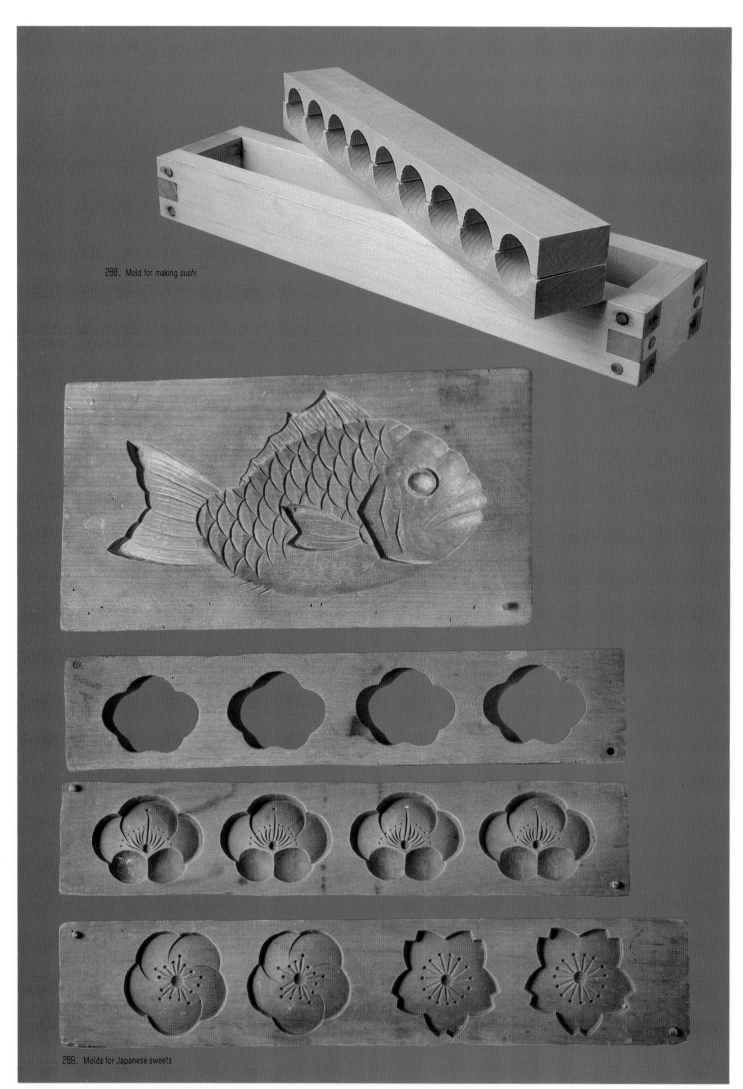

288. Mold for making *sushi*

289. Molds for Japanese sweets

122

290. Rice scoop

291. Rice scoop

292. Soup ladle

293. Soup ladle

294. Wooden cooking utensil

295. *Morite* (scoop for noodles)

296. Mortar

297. Stone mill

BASKETS AND
MEASURE BOXES
筬・升

The workman's art is reflected in baskets and winnows of finely woven bamboo or rattan. Hung in the corner of a kitchen or shed, these baskets and wooden measuring boxes silently remind us of the help they have given people.

299. Bamboo basket

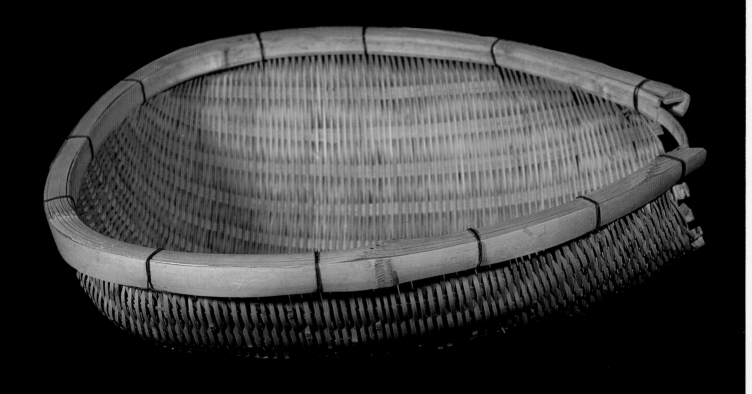

300. Round bamboo basket

301. Bamboo strainer

302. Round, flat bamboo basket

127

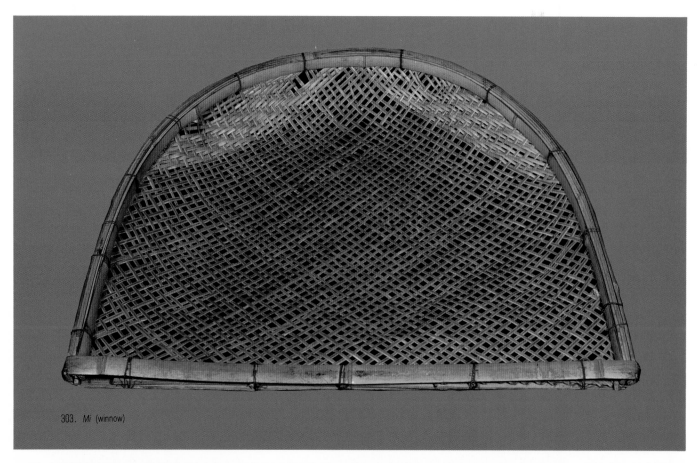

303. *Mi* (winnow)

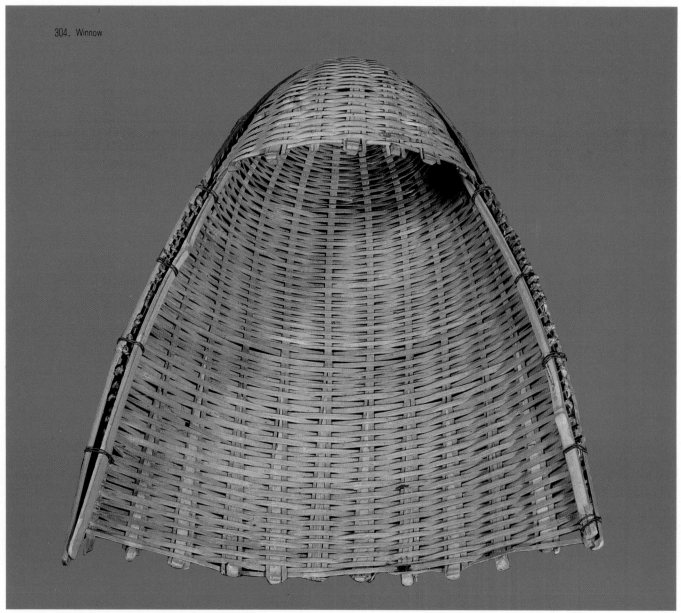

304. Winnow

305. Bamboo funnel

306. Bamboo basket

307. Measure

308. Measure with handle

309. Round measure

The tradition of offering food to the gods has a long history. There were times when it was hard to produce or buy enough food to feed one's family. Embodied in the solemn form of utensil is a thanksgiving for the blessings of nature and a prayer for a fertile earth.

310. *Sanbō* (stand for offerings of food)

312. Decorations attached to saké bottles

313. Bottle for *miki* (saké offered to the gods)

314. Rice scoops given as an offering

315. Articles for Shinto rites held in a rice field

135

316. Papers pasted on kitchen wall bearing words for protection against fire

Glossary

akae: *see* overglaze enamel

Akaraku: hand-molded pottery (*rakuyaki*) with a reddish-brown overglaze

Akazu (Akazu-*yaki*, Akazu ware): pottery, mostly teaware, made in the Akazu section of Seto City, Aichi Prefecture

ash-glazed *(haigusuri)*: descriptive of an overglaze in which ashes of plant matter are the main component

bentō-bako: a box for a *bentō*, or packed lunch

Bizen (Bizen-*yaki*, Bizen ware): stoneware from the Bizen region (now Bizen City) of Okayama Prefecture, characterized by its dark brown and black color

blue-underglazed: a translation of *sometsuke*, a process in which an object of pottery to be fired is printed with white glaze over which a pattern containing cobalt oxide is painted. A clear glaze is painted over this, and the object is fired. The finished product displays the pattern in blue. The process originated in China during the Yüan dynasty (1271–1368) and arrived in Arita, Kyushu, in the early 1600s. Also, an object made by this process.

bon: a tray with a shallow rim; round, square, or in another shape; made of wood, metal, bamboo, or other material

chagama: a kettle used in the tea ceremony, or any kettle used for boiling tea

chaire: a general term for a tea container

chasen: a whip for stirring up powdered tea (*matcha*) in hot water

chashaku: a long-handled spoon of wood, bamboo, ivory, lacquer, etc., used in the tea ceremony for scooping powdered tea (*matcha*)

chataku: a saucer for teacups

chawan (in compounds, *jawan*): although the term literally means "tea bowl," it refers collectively to teacups and rice bowls, and sometimes to pottery with an overglaze in general

chazutsu: a tea canister, one kind of *chaire*

chiri-renge **(lit., "scattered lotus petal")**: a china spoon whose shape is reminiscent of a lotus petal

choko **(also, *choku*)**: (1) a small saké cup with a base wider than its mouth; (2) a small bowl of the same shape as (1) used in a formal Japanese meal for *sashimi*, vinegared foods, and the like (see also *soba choko*)

chōshi: a long-handled pitcher of metal or wood for pouring saké, with one or two spouts. Vessels for warming saké are also called *chōshi*.

dōban sometsuke **(see also blue under-glazed)**: a process in which paper painted with cobalt oxide in a desired pattern is attached to a ceramic object to be fired. The paper burns off in the kiln, leaving the pattern in blue on the object. Also, a ceramic object made by this process.

dobin: a clay tea kettle

Eshino: a form of Shino ware (*see* Shino) with painted figures in an iron-based under-glaze

hachi (in compounds, -*bachi*): a bowl, usually of ceramic, shallower than a *wan* and with a wide upper part

Hagi (Hagi-*yaki*, Hagi ware): pottery from Hagi and Nagato cities, Yamaguchi Prefecture, originally brought over from Korea. A glaze containing straw ashes is used.

haisen: a bowl containing water for washing saké cups

hakeme: a glaze pattern made by spreading white enamel on the object and covering this with an overglaze

hanki: a wooden lacquered rice bowl

hanzo: a water pitcher whose handle goes halfway inside the body of the pitcher

heishi **(also *heiji*)**: a *tokuri* with a wide shoulder and narrow base and mouth, originally made in the Heian period. Early *heishi* were of lacquerware, later ones of metal and ceramic.

Hidehira-*wan*: large black-lacquered bowls with plants and cranes painted on them in red lacquer, from Iwate Prefecture. Perhaps named after Fujiwara Hidehira (nobleman, ?–1187).

ichimatsu **(*ichimatsu moyō*, *ichimatsu* pattern)**: a checkerboard pattern

inrō: a seal case; a pillbox

iroe: *see* overglaze enamel

ishiusu: a stone mill

jūbako: a nest, or tier, of boxes made of wood, ceramic, or other material, used for holding prepared food. Two-, three-, and five-tiered *jūbako* are common.

kama (in compounds, -*gama*): a kettle; an iron pot

kamado: a stove made of earth, stone, brick, or other material

Kamakura carving: a technique in which a wood carving is painted with ordinary lacquer, or with red and green lacquer. It was done in imitation of a similar technique from China and came to Japan during the Muromachi period.

kame: a wide, deep ceramic or metal pot

kasane-wan: a set of bowls made to be stacked together

katakuchi: a bowl (*hachi*) with a spout for pouring saké, soy sauce, etc.

kioke: a wooden bucket (*oke*)

kōgō: a lidded incense container of lacquerware, a ceramic, shell, or other material

kohiki: a Korean form of pottery whose white overglaze appears as if there is flour in it

koma: a form of Chinese lacquerware in which red, yellow, and green lacquer are painted in concentric circles on the object. Originally found in the Ming dynasty, it came to Japan in the Edo period.

komedawara: a large straw bag for rice

kōro: an incense burner made of metal, ceramic, lacquerware, or other material, in various shapes. It was originally a Buddhist implement, but is now used more generally; in a tea-ceremony house it decorates the alcove.

Koseto: pottery made in the Seto area (now Seto City) of Aichi Prefecture. Its overglaze often contains ashes (*see* ash-glazed)

kuromoji yōji: a large toothpick (*yōji*) made of the spicebush (*kuromoji*), put out with sweets at the tea ceremony

Kutani (Kutani-*yaki*, Kutani ware): pottery from Komatsu City and nearby areas of Ishikawa Prefecture, noted for its colorful pictures

Kyūsu: a ceramic teapot, or a small clay one (*dobin*) with a metal handle

magewappa: a round wooden container for food, made by softening thin pieces of wood and bending them into shape

makie: a process, begun in the Nara period, in which a pattern is painted on an object with lacquer, and while the lacquer is still wet, gold or silver powder (or other colored powder) is sprinkled onto it

mamezara: a small dish (*sara*) for seasonings and side dishes

masu: a container of wood or metal, round or square, for measuring grain, saké, oil, etc.

masuhai: a wooden saké cup in the shape of a measure (*masu*)

meshibitsu: a lidded wooden rice tub, either round or oval

meshigama: a kettle (*kama*) for boiling rice

meshi-jawan: a bowl (*chawan*) from which rice is eaten; a rice bowl

mi: a tool for separating chaff from grain; a winnow

Miho-no-Matsubara: a windbreak of pines on the Miho peninsula, Shizuoka Prefecture, noted for its beautiful view of Mount Fuji

miki: saké given in offering to the gods

miki kazari: decorative ornaments inserted in the mouths of bottles of *miki*

mitsu-gasane-wan: a set of three *kasane-wan*

mizusashi: a container, used in the tea ceremony, in which water for rinsing teacups and utensils is placed

mokkō: a crest, rhomboid in shape, that resembles an egg in the center of a nest

mokuhai: a wooden saké cup

morite: a pronged scoop for putting noodles into a bowl

mukōzuke: the items of food placed on the side of the tray away from the person eating (as opposed to the rice and soup, which are placed on the tray immediately in front of the eater). Also, the dishes used for these foods.

nabe: a metal or ceramic cooking pot, usually round and shallower than a *kama* (kettle)

natsume: a jujube, or Chinese date; a lacquerware tea container (*chaire*) in the shape of this fruit, used for holding powdered tea (*matcha*) in the tea ceremony

Negoro (Negoro-*nuri*, Negoro-lacquered): a form of lacquerware originating during the Muromachi period at Negoro Temple, Wakayama Prefecture, in which an object is painted with several layers of black lacquer over which red lacquer is then painted

Nezumishino: Shino ware the color of a mouse (*nezumi*), i.e., grayish

nuri: painted; often used specifically to mean lacquered; used as a suffix

o-hitsu: a lidded wooden container for cooked rice, in the shape of a bucket

okamochi: a shallow tub with a handle, used for carrying food

oke: a wooden tub or bucket

Oribe (Oribe-*yaki*, Oribe ware): pottery of the Mino group named after the master Furuta Oribe and known for its original shapes and patterns

oshiki: a square tray (*bon*) with or without beveled corners, with edges made of thin shavings of Japanese cedar or Japanese cypress

overglaze enamel: a translation of two terms, *akae* (''red picture,'' *akae* in the captions) and *iroe* (''colored picture,'' *iroe* in the captions.) *Akae* refers to colored overglaze designs, predominantly red; *iroe* is the more general term, referring to overglaze designs in various colors.

pine-bamboo-plum (*sho-chiku-bai*): called the ''three friends of winter'' because they withstand the cold of that season (pine and bamboo remaining green, and plum blooming), these plants are used together in artwork, decorative greetings, etc.

sahari: an alloy of 10 parts copper, 2 parts lead, and 1 part tin used for pitchers, kettles, and bowls. Objects made with it make a nice sound when tapped.

sakazuki: a cup for drinking saké, originally of unglazed earthenware, now of lacquerware, ceramic, metal, glass, or other material

saketsugi: a saké pitcher

sanbō: a wooden stand for offering food to the gods. It is made of a tray (*oshiki*) placed atop a stand, three of whose sides contain a hole.

sara: a flat, shallow food dish or plate of ceramic, glass, metal, lacquerware, or other material

sashidaru: a saké flask in the shape of an upright flattened box, used on ceremonial occasions

seigaiha: a pattern of blue overlapping waves used on fabrics and elsewhere

seiro: a square or round wood-framed container with a latticework bottom, placed over a kettle to steam foods

sendanmaki: the pattern created when a string or rattan is wrapped around an object; originally used for spear handles and the like

shakushi: a flat scoop for rice or a soup ladle

shifuku: a bag for tea containers (*chaire*), teacups, etc., often of gold brocade or damask

Shigaraki (Shigaraki-*yaki*, Shigaraki ware): pottery from the Shigaraki region of Shiga Prefecture, known for its rough texture

shinnari: ''true shape.'' A *shinnari* kettle is a basic ''kettle-shaped'' kettle.

Shino (Shino-*yaki*, Shino ware): pottery from Gifu Prefecture covered heavily with a glaze containing feldspar

shippō-tsunagi: a pattern of overlapping ellipses

Shunkei (Shunkei-*nuri*, Shunkei-lacquered): a lacquering method originating in the Osaka area. The wood is treated with persimmon juice to prevent the lacquer from penetrating it. Clear lacquer is painted over this, and the grain of the wood shows through

soba choko: a small bowl (see *choko*) into which the water left over from boiling *soba* (buckwheat noodles) is put (this liquid is drunk)

sometsuke: see blue-underglazed

suichū: in the tea ceremony, a pitcher for pouring water into the *mizusashi*

suitō: a water container suitable for carrying on a walk; a canteen

suribachi: a ceramic mortar with finely etched lines on the inside surface for grinding such foods as *miso* and sesame seeds

Takasago: a scenic area of Hyogo Prefecture noted for its double pine

takasara: a plate on a stand

takatsuki: a tray with a tall, thin stand

Tanba (Tanba-*yaki*; Tanba ware): pottery from the former Tanba Province (corresponding today to parts of Kyoto and Hyogo prefectures) made in various styles and with various techniques during different historical periods

tebachi: a bowl (*hachi*) with a handle

tenmoku: a relatively shallow teacup used in the tea ceremony

tenmokudai: a stand for tea offered to the gods or ancestors

Tokoname (Tokoname-*yaki*, Tokoname ware): stoneware from Tokoname City, Aichi Prefecture, used mostly for such daily-use objects as *tsubo* and pots

tokuri (also, *tokkuri*): a tall, narrow saké bottle with a narrow mouth, of ceramic, glass, metal, or other material

tsubo: a vessel of ceramic, wood, metal, or other material with a large body and relatively small mouth; an urn

tsugura: a woven-straw basket for keeping a rice tub (*meshibitsu*) warm

tsunodaru: a saké keg with two handles shaped like horns (*tsuno*) on the sides, usually black—or red—lacquered; used as a gift

tsutsu-jawan: a cylindrical-shaped teacup (*chawan*)

umamome-zara ("horse's eye" plate): a large plate painted with swirl patterns resembling a horse's eye. They ceased being made during the Meiji period.

uzukumaru (lit., "to squat"): a small, squat *tsubo*, originally used on farms for beans, tea, oil, etc.

Wajima (Wajima-*nuri*, Wajima-lacquered): Lacquerware from the Wajima region of Ishikawa Prefecture, noted for its gold and *makie* patterns.

wan: a bowl of wood, ceramic, metal, etc.

-yaki: "fired," "burned"; used as a suffix meaning (pottery) ware

yunomi: short for *yunomi-jawan* (see *chawan*); a teacup

yutō: a wooden pitcher, usually lacquered, used to hold hot water or tea drunk after a meal

yuzamashi: a vessel for cooling hot water

zen: a tray, usually with legs, for serving food

zonsei: a lacquerware technique perhaps originally used in Ming dynasty China and brought to Japan during the Edo period. A design is either painted on with colored lacquer or carved into the object, after which carved parts are filled with colored lacquer.